men and women in marriage

A document from the Faith and Order Commission
published with the agreement of the House of Bishops
of the Church of England and approved for study

GS Misc 1046

CHURCH HOUSE
PUBLISHING

Church House Publishing
Church House
Great Smith Street
London SW1P 3AZ

ISBN: 978 0 7151 4373 5

This document is issued by the Faith and Order Commission of the Church
of England at the request of the Standing Committee of the House of Bishops.

Published in 2013 for the Faith and Order Commission of the General Synod
of the Church of England by Church House Publishing

Printed in the UK

contents

foreword

Last year the Faith and Order Commission suggested to the Standing Committee of the House of Bishops that it would be timely to produce a short summary of the Church of England's understanding of marriage. The Standing Committee agreed.

A draft from the Commission was considered by the House of Bishops at its meeting in December. The House welcomed it, invited the Commission to take account of its discussion in producing a final text of the document and authorized the Standing Committee to approve its publication on its behalf. The Standing Committee did so on 13 March.

This document from the Faith and Order Commission is published with the agreement of the House and commended for study. It sets out to explain the continued importance of and rationale for the doctrine of the Church of England on marriage as set out in *The Book of Common Prayer*, Canon B30, the *Common Worship* Marriage Service and the teaching document issued by the House in September 1999.

✠ Justin Cantuar: ✠ Sentamu Ebor:

April 2013

men and women in marriage

The purpose of this document

1. When the British Government held a consultation in the spring of 2012 on projected legislation for same-sex marriage, the Church of England replied that it could not support the idea. The arguments were set out in its response, and this document does not propose to repeat them. The disagreements now need to be set against a more positive background of how Christians have understood and valued marriage.

2. In 2005 the Bishops stated the Church of England's position in these words: 'marriage is a creation ordinance, a gift of God in creation and a means of his grace. Marriage, defined as a faithful, committed, permanent and legally sanctioned relationship between a man and a woman, is central to the stability and health of human society. It continues to provide the best context for the raising of children.'[1]

3. What follows is intended to enlarge on that summary, drawing on what has been said by the Church of England historically and more recently, and especially on how the sexual differentiation of men and women is a gift of God, who 'created humankind in his image... male and female he created them'. It is on male and female that God gives his blessing, which is to be seen not only in procreation but in human culture, too (Genesis 1.27-8).[2]

4.   Marriage, like most important undertakings of life, can be lived
      more successfully or less successfully. Mistakes are made, by
      couples, by their friends and relatives, and sometimes also by
      pastors and institutions of the church, and these can be costly in
      human terms. Lack of clear understanding of marriage can only
      multiply disappointments and frustrations. Public discussion at this
      juncture needs a clear view of why Christians believe and act in
      relation to marriage as they do, and this statement is offered as
      a resource for that.

Belief in God the Creator

5.   The Church of England's *Common Worship* Marriage Service
      declares, 'Marriage is a gift of God in creation'. The teaching of
      Jesus on marriage began with creation: 'he who created them at the
      beginning made them male and female, and said, "Therefore a man
      shall leave his father and his mother and hold fast to his wife, and
      the two shall become one flesh"' (Matthew 19.4-5 (ESV)).

6.   In calling it a *gift of God*, we mean that it is not simply a cultural
      development (though it has undergone much cultural development)
      nor simply a political or economic institution (though often
      embedded in political and economic arrangements). It is an
      expression of the human nature which God has willed for us and
      which we share. And although marriage may fall short of God's
      purposes in many ways and be the scene of many human
      weaknesses, it receives the blessing of God and is included

2

in his judgment that creation is 'very good' (Genesis 1.31). In calling it a gift of God *in creation*, we view marriage within its wider life-context: as an aspect of human society and as a structure of life that helps us shape our journey from birth to death.

7. God is the 'maker of heaven and earth'; his good purpose governs all that is, and the Church's first task is to praise God for that. Christian understanding, like Jewish, seeks to discern the goodness of God in the natural world, a universe of good things, good not only in themselves but in their relations to each other.

8. All that is most important in art and science, all that is intelligible and beautiful, depends on discernments of a similar kind: the artist who reflects a fragment of experience back to us in a new way, the scientist who captures complex observations in a formula that renders them intelligible. The marvellous ordering of the created world has not lost its force for a generation made more aware than before by discoveries in physics and biology of the dynamic unfolding of the universe, the interplay between innovation and constancy, variation and intelligibility.

9. When the ancient creation narrative spoke of God's work as 'completed' (Genesis 2.1 (NIV)), it did not mean that the creative power had exhausted itself, but that God's ongoing activity was consistent with what he had given. Christians have spoken of God's 'faithfulness' to his creation, as they have found in it a structure of intelligibility capable of being appreciated by all, a 'natural law'.

10.   There is a eucharistic prayer that relates our human life strikingly to its cosmic and ecological context: 'At your command all things came to be: the vast expanse of interstellar space, galaxies, suns, the planets in their courses, and this fragile earth, our island home'.[3] Human beings inhabit this vast expanse, and are also part of it. We, too, are 'fragile earth', of the material world. Not everything in the way we live, then, is open to renegotiation. We cannot turn our back upon the natural, and especially the biological, terms of human existence.

11.   The vocation of being human in all its dimensions, social, cultural, intellectual and spiritual, rests on the distinctive form of nature we humans are given. We share with many animal species the sexual differentiation of male and female, serving the tasks of reproduction and the nurture of children, but we do more than share it; we build on it to enhance the bond between the sexes culturally.

12.   Human relations depend on the encounter of men and women, equally and differently human, offering each other social fulfilment and placing their endowments of emotion and perception at each other's service. As Saint Paul writes, 'woman is not independent of man nor man of woman' (1 Corinthians 11.11 (ESV)). To flourish as individuals we need a society in which men and women relate well to each other.

Marriage and society

13.   Humans are elaborately social, depending on one another to a high degree, cooperating and communicating distinctively through the gift of language. Marriage is only one form of society, but a central one. 'The first blessing God gave to man was society,' wrote Jeremy Taylor in the seventeenth century, 'and that society was a marriage', suggesting that marriage is a paradigm of society, facilitating other social forms.[4]

14.   Every human being will be involved in social relations with members of both the same and the other sex, some close and some distant, and the successful living of life requires an ability to form and conduct both kinds of relation well. This does not mean that every human being is called to be married. The Church has long learned to value the calling to live unmarried, whether under vows or not, for the sake of a more undivided attention to the service of God and humanity.

15.   Yet both married and unmarried have a stake in the health of marriage as a factor in the health of society. In the words of the *Common Worship* Marriage Service, marriage 'enriches society and strengthens community'.

16.   It is possible to lose sight of the social importance of marriage. In some cultural periods it has been seen as inferior to an ascetic life, in others it has been romanticized. It has sometimes appeared an

irrelevance where serious economic, political or intellectual tasks are in question. It has also been valued in unbalanced ways. The flexibility and supportiveness of marriage depend on an integration of its various elements, for it is a thread woven of many strands: it satisfies the needs of youth, assists the cooperative venture of parenthood, strengthens the role of memory in old age, and so on. What is important is the way these strands are spun together to give the thread a strength that is more than the sum of its parts.

17.   Certain basic structural features make marriage the flexible and supportive social institution it is. It is an alliance outside the close family circle (technically called 'exogamy'), so that a partnership of natural kinship-groups is formed in transmitting human life to new generations. It is undertaken for the full length of a couple's life. And it is an exclusive commitment of one man and one woman.

18.   This understanding of marriage, common to Christians and Jews, is distinctive but not idiosyncratic. Most developed traditions give these three structural elements a central place in their practices of marriage.

19.   There have been cultures (the patriarchal period of the Old Testament among them) in which compromises have been accepted especially over exogamy and monogamy, but these compromises have tended to be of limited scope. It is possible to exaggerate the cultural relativity of marriage-forms. Many differences there have been, but they hardly amount to a significant challenge to these structural foundations.

6

20. The principle of marrying outside the family has not been very controversial in modern liberal societies, where unmarried men and women are usually free to move in wider social circles. The lifelong intention of marriage, on the other hand, has raised many questions. The Bishops of the Church of England wrote on it in some detail in 1999 in the context of debates about the marriage of the divorced in a church ceremony.

Parenthood and partnership

21. But it is now the principle of union between one man and one woman that requires closer attention. When we marry, we commit the procreative power of our own sex to an exclusive relation with a life-partner of the opposite sex. We open ourselves to parenthood in and through the partnership we enjoy as a couple, and that may be true even of a couple who, for whatever reasons, have no prospect of actually having children.

22. This was emphasized by the Lambeth Conference in 1930, when it affirmed the 'duty of parenthood as the glory of married life', not meaning that the married partnership was subordinated to parenthood, but that the two complemented and crowned each other.[5] We are (potentially or actually) parents as we are wife and husband, not parents on the one hand and husband or wife on the other. Any children we may have are 'ours' together, not 'yours and mine' separately, ours both through the biological bond and through

the bond of family love that springs from the partnership, each bond strengthening the other.

23. This does not mean, of course, that only an ideal family unit of two biological parents can provide a home for children. Society has good reason to be grateful to adoptive parents and step-parents, as also to single parents who must sometimes undertake heroic struggles. But the struggles underline the point: they would be less, other things being equal, and the child more securely placed, had it grown up within the marriage-bond of its mother and father.

24. When a single mother says to her children, 'I have to be both mother and father to you!' she recognizes the need to supply the place of the absent father, and teaches her children, at the same time, to look for something more in their home than she can give as a single mother. Furthermore, for children to grow up in some other home than their parents' may in some circumstances, be their best hope of a secure childhood. But a good alternative will imitate as closely as possible the form it seeks to substitute for.

25. Our age prides itself on appreciating marriage supremely as a relationship between persons. But the intimate personal relationship is not simply detachable from the wider set of social relationships. Persons in relation are not interchangeable units, shorn of whatever makes one human being different from another. They are individuals who bring to

the relationship unique experiences of being human in community, unique qualities, attributes and histories.

26. Biological differences do not simply cease to matter at the level of personal relationship; persons are not asexual, but are either male or female. Their sex attains a personal meaning, as relationships are built constructively on the endowments and strengths it offers. The relationship of marriage is more personal, not less, as the partners come to it in receptiveness of what only the opposite sex can bring to their own.

Freedom and growth

27. All human existence involves a dynamic interplay of nature and freedom; our natural powers are the foundation on which we can exercise our freedom effectively. In every sphere of life, and not only in marriage, we face questions about how freedom can be used constructively, not undermining its own foundations.

28. The ecological debates of our age illustrate how the perception of the world as a balanced and well-calibrated order, on the one hand, and the perception of it as a theatre of exploration and innovation on the other, need to be held closely together, correcting and informing each other. When the Bible declares that God made the first human beings 'in the image of God' and as 'male and female' (Genesis 1.27), it draws the principles of nature and freedom together.

29. In God's image we bring spiritual creativity to our natural endowment without denying or overthrowing it. As male and female we have a foundation for growth, cultural development, moral responsibility, intellectual and practical fulfilment, and for the end to which God summons us individually and together, worship and fellowship with himself.

30. This cooperation of nature and freedom is embodied especially in marriage. Its disciplines are not a mere constraint, a form we must accept and conform to somehow; it is a 'vocation to holiness', a path of discipleship by which we are opened to the life of the Spirit of God in the context of material existence.[6]

31. It is 'one of the central means through which the continuation of the development of the personality occurs,' offering 'healing and growth on the basis of progressive mutual completion'.[7] The role of binding and public promises in the making of marriage is itself a summons to mature responsibility, said the Bishops in 1999, requiring 'courage' while yet being 'liberating'.[8]

32. The support marriage offers to spiritual growth is expressed in an ancient account, derived from St Augustine and adopted by the Church of England as well as by other churches, of 'three ends' of marriage: offspring, faithfulness and sacramental union. These 'ends' are not envisaged as particular goals or objects in marrying, but as 'blessings that belong to marriage'.[9]

33.   They were conceived originally as reflecting in some sense the
       spiritual growth of a married couple in the course of life: the physical
       good of the shared role in procreation laid the foundation for a moral
       responsibility towards each other, in turn allowing the union to attain
       a permanence which could speak to the world of God's own love.
       Taken together they describe the cultural bridge which marriage
       builds between the basic physical needs of our species and its
       spiritual vocation.

34.   The good of offspring, the service of marriage to the transmission
       of the human race, goes far beyond simple biological reproduction.
       Parents initiate the care, education and equipment of their children
       for the moral and spiritual tasks of life, bringing them up, as *The
       Book of Common Prayer* expresses it, 'in the fear and nurture of
       the Lord and to the praise of his holy Name'.

35.   Marriage thus plays a central role in the transmission of human
       culture and the life of the church itself. Not less significant is the
       emotional education that parents convey to their young children not
       only by the comfort offered as they learn to inhabit their bodies and
       by patient affection in the tumultuous stresses of growing up, but
       also in the way they live out before the children the strength of a
       shared life in coping with disagreements and disappointments.
       These various goods rely in different ways on the complementary
       gifts of men and women.

36.　The 'hallowing and right direction of natural instincts and affections' is how Anglicans in recent generations have expressed the second of the three goods, the good of faithfulness.[10] This balances, but does not deny, an emphasis upon the turbulence of human instincts expressed in the classical phrase, used in *The Book of Common Prayer*, 'remedy for sin'. It is not only sexual instincts that are in view here, but those of competition and censorious judgment, which may contribute to anti-social dynamics in the personality that can poison male-female relations.[11]

37.　The disciplines of marital faithfulness help bring these to order. They provide a way of sanctification and moral development, and draw from the partnership of male and female a capacity for each to take responsibility for the other, a responsibility from which it is too easy to shy away. Contrasting contributions, when seen through the eyes of a close affection, can be opportunities for each to make good what the other lacks, over time and throughout life, and turn mutual frustration into mutual help.

38.　And how should sacramental union be understood? 'Sacrament' was a description of marriage of which the Anglican Reformers fought shy for good reasons at the time, but which has come to be valued, as the Bishops said, though it 'does not have exactly the same sense as when it is applied to the two "sacraments of the Gospel", baptism and eucharist'.[12]

39. The Epistle to the Ephesians (5.32) describes marriage as a 'mystery' applied to Christ and the Church, and this word, translated into Latin as sacramentum, was generally understood to mean a concrete sign of God's saving work for humanity. In expressing the third good in the marriage service as 'the mutual society, help, and comfort, that the one ought to have of the other, both in prosperity and adversity', *The Book of Common Prayer* also referred to this biblical passage. The *Common Worship* service elaborates: 'as man and woman grow together in love and trust, they shall be united with one another in heart, body and mind, as Christ is united with his bride, the Church'.

40. The encounter of man and woman in marriage affords an image, then, of the knowledge and love of God, to which all humans are summoned, and of the self-giving of the Son of God which makes it possible.

State and Church in relation to marriage

41. Neither the state nor the Church can claim a prior right over marriage, nor does either of them 'make' marriages, which is done by God's providence working through the public promises of the couples themselves.

42. Since the dawn of the modern era it has been accepted that the regulation of formalities was a proper task for the state in its general

concern to protect against abuse and injustice. The precise extent to which the state became involved in marriage has varied from country to country subsequently. In England (apart from the Commonwealth period) marriage remained an important element in Canon Law, and when in the nineteenth century civil marriage ceremonies were first introduced to Britain, great care was taken to keep their understanding of marriage consonant with inherited Christian understanding.

43. The greater involvement of the state was never understood to mean that there were two kinds of marriage, a 'religious' and a 'civil' marriage, with different laws appropriate to each. There have simply been two kinds of marriage ceremony. Correspondingly, the Church has generally not questioned the reality of marriages performed in civil ceremonies.

44. Not all who marry are Christians. The Church guards a common traditional understanding of marriage as a human, not only a religious act.[13] In presiding over the making of Christian marriages, it also points to how marriage is a form of committed Christian discipleship for those who understand their own love as part of God's love towards the world.

45. The mission of the Church – not only in relation to marriage but with other perennial features of human life like birth and death, and with social structures, too, as in an act of civic worship – is to teach the Gospel by proclaiming God's goodness in creation and redemption

and by giving pastoral help to those who seek to engage with the challenges of life responsibly.

46. There is in all these cases a doctrinal and a pastoral aspect to the Church's mission: speaking the truth about God and his works, and making that truth the basis for concrete practical engagements. In relation to marriage in particular the Church's tasks are both doctrinal and pastoral, to draw attention to the source and purpose of marriage and to 'solemnize' it, incorporating it into the sacramental community of the Gospel, offering help, wherever it is welcome, to those who are approaching marriage.

47. In pastoral responses a degree of flexibility may be called for in finding ways to express the Church's teaching practically. In affirming its belief in marriage as the form the Creator has given us for intimate and permanent relationship of a man and a woman, the Church does not treat questions of what is possible in hard circumstances or exceptional conditions as simply closed. They require pastoral wisdom.

48. In opting a decade ago for a provision for marriage after divorce, for example, the Church of England maintained the principles 'that marriage is an unconditional commitment for life' and 'that a further marriage after a divorce is an exceptional act'. In this context it sought to offer pastoral support to those who 'with great honesty and circumspection' approached a further marriage.[14] The African Churches had earlier taken an initiative to help baptismal

candidates who were in polygamous family units to fulfil their
responsibilities without compromising the norm of monogamy.
With regard to civil partnerships, which are not marriages but raise
some analogous issues, the Bishops addressed what might be
an appropriate form of pastoral response in 2005.[15] The wider
questions surrounding these continue to be a matter of study.

49.   The meaning of such pastoral accommodations can be
       misunderstood, as though the Church were solving pastoral
       difficulties by redefining marriage from the ground up, which it
       cannot do. What it can do is devise accommodations for specific
       conditions, bearing witness in special ways to the abiding
       importance of the norm. Well-designed accommodations proclaim
       the form of life given by God's creative goodness and bring those
       in difficult positions into closer approximation to it. They mark the
       point where teaching and pastoral care coincide.

50.   It has seemed to some that the disagreement over same-sex
       marriage is a disagreement over mere names. But names govern
       how we think, and how we think governs what we learn to
       appreciate. When marriage is spoken of unclearly or misleadingly, it
       distorts the way couples try to conduct their relationship and makes
       for frustration and disappointment. The reality of marriage between
       one man and one woman will not disappear as the result of any
       legislative change, for God has given this gift, and it will remain part
       of our created human endowment. But the disciplines of living in it
       may become more difficult to acquire, and the path to fulfilment, in
       marriage and in other relationships, more difficult to find.

notes

1. *Civil Partnerships: A Pastoral Statement from the House of Bishops*, 2005, para. 2. A doctrinal statement is also incorporated in the legal setting of Canon B30, stating 'according to our Lord's teaching' that marriage 'is in its nature a union permanent and life-long, for better for worse, till death do them part, of one man with one woman'.
2. In *The Book of Common Prayer* the polarity is emphasized in one of the blessings upon the couple: 'Send thy blessing upon these thy servants, this man and this woman, whom we bless in thy Name'.
3. *The Book of Common Prayer*, according to the use of the Episcopal Church of America, 1979.
4. Jeremy Taylor, 'The Marriage Ring, or, the Mysteriousness and Duties of Marriage', from *Twenty-Five Sermons*, 1653.
5. Lambeth Conference 1930, Resolution 14.
6. Lambeth Conference 1958, Resolution 113.
7. *Marriage, Divorce and the Church*, SPCK, 1971, paras 36, 40.
8. *Marriage: a Teaching Document from the House of Bishops of the Church of England*, Church House Publishing, 1999, p. 10.
9. *Marriage*, 1999, p. 8.
10. Most recently in Canon B30.
11. The Elizabethan *Homily on Marriage* gave special attention to the role of marriage both in addressing various personal forms of disintegration and in overcoming a tendency in the two sexes to misunderstanding and mistrust, laying at each other's door the blame for deterioration in their relationship. This sensitive piece of instruction from the sixteenth century was put together from ecumenical sources, Lutheran and Greek.
12. *Marriage*, 1999, p. 13. Cf. *An Honourable Estate*, Church House Publishing, 1988, para. 42: 'The two complementary aspects of the teaching of the Church of England, the stress on creation and on the sacramental character of marriage, set the boundaries of our doctrine.'
13. *An Honourable Estate* stated (para. 26): 'The choice is between either taking up a doctrine of Christian marriage and leaving the others to go their own way, or pursuing a Christian understanding of marriage which is applicable to everyone. The doctrine and practice of the Church of England has long held to the second of these two approaches.'
14. *Marriage*, 1999, p. 18.
15. *Civil Partnerships: A Pastoral Statement from the House of Bishops*, para. 18: 'Where clergy are approached by people asking for prayer in relation to entering into a civil partnership, they should respond pastorally and sensitively in the light of the circumstances of each case.'

17

further reading

The Book of Common Prayer, 'The Form of Solemnization of Matrimony' (http://www.churchofengland.org/prayer-worship/worship/book-of-common-prayer/the-form-of-solemnization-of-matrimony.aspx).

Common Worship: Marriage, Church House Publishing, 2000 (http://www.churchofengland.org/prayer-worship/worship/texts/pastoral/marriage.aspx).

The Canons of the Church of England (Seventh Edition), Church House Publishing, 2012, Canon B.30 (http://www.churchofengland.org/about-us/structure/churchlawlegis/canons/).

Civil Partnerships: A Pastoral Statement from the House of Bishops, 2005 (http://www.churchofengland.org/media-centre/news/2005/07/pr5605.aspx).

'An Homily of the State of Matrimony,' in I. Robinson (Ed.), *The Homilies*, Brynmill/ Preservation Press, 2006.

An Honourable Estate, Church House Publishing, 1988.

Marriage: a Teaching Document from the House of Bishops of the Church of England, Church House Publishing, 1999.

Marriage, Divorce and the Church, SPCK, 1971.

Jeremy Taylor, 'The Marriage Ring, or, the Mysteriousness and Duties of Marriage' in *Jeremy Taylor Selected Works*, Paulist Press, 1990 (http://www.prnd.ca/PRNDmarriagetaylor.html).